OUTRAGEOUS DREAMER

Conquer fear
Chase your dream
Create a life you LOVE

JOSEPH FOSTER

Printed in the United States.
Printed by: Outrageous Living | Morrisville, NC
Project Management: Start Write, LLC | Raindrop Brand

CONTENTS

INTRODUCTION

We are living in the most amazing time in history. People who have lost their jobs are making six figures within one year of starting their own businesses. Women and other minorities are being elected into public office at record numbers and rising to the ranks in C-level positions of Fortune 500 companies. Yet, at the same time, people are struggling and fighting for decent living wages. Millions are facing being left without health insurance (in the wake of political changes), and millions are depending on the government for retirement in a time where there are drastic changes being made to the Social Security and Medicaid systems. Older people are not the only ones struggling. All generations are burdened with student loan debt, with many of those graduates unable to find a job in their field of study.

I am not sure whether you are living your best life or in the middle of your toughest struggle. Either way, I have taken the time to let you know that no matter where you are in life; there is more in store for you.

How do you know? Because there is a dream that is inside of you that you have not birthed yet. That dream is connected to your purpose. That dream is the vehicle to your destiny, and I want to help you release it from Dream Jail.

Dream Jail is where dreams get stuck; it is where the trials and detours of your life sentence them to die. Well, if the Bible's ultimate dreamer, Joseph, can be released from Dream Jail, you can too.

Genesis 37 outlines the beginning of Joseph's troubles. He is his father's favorite, and it is not secret. In addition to not having to work as hard as his brothers, his father lavishes his love on Joseph by gifting him with a coat of many colors. To add insult to injury, Joseph shares his dreams with them, which foreshadow his ruling over them all. This was the final straw for his brothers. They decided that something must be done about their "coat-of-many-colors dreaming brother." Narrowly escaping death, Joseph is sold into slavery.

Now, as grim as this part of Joseph's story is; it should minister to anyone who has felt like they have been wrongly treated. In fact, this is the first lesson we learn from Joseph:

Joseph's dream was greater than his adversity.

Joseph was sent to Potiphar's house. He worked harder there than he ever had to previously. He was well learned, so he was able to serve administratively as well. Potiphar trusted him with everything in his house and the position of slavery had turned into a managerial role for Joseph, which was definitely a much better role than he could have found himself in, and then another situation arises. Potiphar's wife gets angry at Joseph for refusing her advancements and accuses him of attempted assault. An innocent Joseph once again receives a punishment he does not deserve, and is thrown in jail. Here it seemed as if his dream would surely die. Yet at no point was Joseph bitter or angry. In fact, Joseph made every place he entered better than before his arrival. He became a favorite of the warden, and soon the warden placed Joseph in charge of the inmates. This appointment could never have happened without Joseph maintaining his composure although he had been wronged.

Joseph's dream powered his vision and fueled his commitment.

Joseph maintained a personal standard of integrity and vision for his life in every circumstance. No matter what happened to him, it did not change his behavior, his character or influence his personal standards. Joseph's situations did not dictate his actions. Rather, Joseph's pain was one of the keys to his greatness. He learned how to endure at a whole new level. He ministered to others in his darkest hours. He never tried to selfishly push his own agenda. Even when those he helped forgot about him, he still kept a servant's heart. Even after interpreting the baker and cupbearer's dreams, he remained in prison two more years. As a result, he was in the right place at the right time and ended up second in command in a Nation that he entered into as a slave. Let that be a message for every foreigner and every minority. God can raise you up in a place that is not your native land. God can use experiences, tests, and trials to give you the tools you need to birth your dream and just like Joseph...

Your dream can save a nation.

Nothing that you have been through is an accident. You surely are not an accident. One or both of your parents decided to have you, but it was God who decided to send you. You are here for a unique purpose, and your dream is tied to the DNA of your purpose and destiny. It may have been years since you thought about your dream. Or you may be someone who thinks about your dream every day; either way, it is time for action! It is time to arise. It is time to get up and align your life with the dream that God has placed within you. It is your time. Take every dream you have and go save a life, a household, a generation and a nation. Joseph's position put him in a prime place to punish those who afflicted him, yet, he chose forgiveness, and lived a peaceful, prosperous life while watching the fulfillment of his dream come to fruition. Do not let your dream die inside of you; someone needs what you have. It is time to arise out of Dream Jail and head to the Palace. I cannot wait to meet you there.

The following pages contain 12 keys to help you navigate your journey as you put your dream into action. Get a journal, take notes, write down the components of your dream and watch God help you manifest it faster than you thought humanly possible.

CHAPTER 1

YOUR DREAM IS THE ANSWER

One night during my weekly prophetic conference call with some influential believers from around the world, the Spirit of the Lord began to speak to me concerning the current economic crisis. The Spirit of the Lord revealed to me that God was getting ready to release a supernatural anointing upon His sons and daughters to obtain wealth through business endeavors. This anointing will pull the church back to a place of influence and affluence as we seek to build successful businesses. As you are reading this book, I want you to understand that you are sitting under an open Heaven. An open Heaven is symbolic of God presenting opportunities for his people to prosper. This is a season of new opportunities for you! Opportunities will be presented to afford you the opportunity to pursue your dream and take your vision from idea to manifestation. It is time to take what is in your heart and put it into your hand.

The key is going to be not to wait to get started. If you wait, you will miss the move of this particular glory cloud. There is an urgency in the Spirit to start now. Whether your aspiration is a cake business or an accounting firm, this book is your prophetic push! You do not have to be overly concerned with the "how." Why? Because when God gives you an opportunity to prosper, He downloads a strategy in your life that will empower you to get the job done.

What you need to do is get your hands on the plow and not look back. You have to keep moving forward. I like how Jesus addresses this revelation in Luke 9:62:

But Jesus told him, "Anyone who lets himself be distracted from the work I plan for him is not fit for the Kingdom of God." (The Living Bible)

When you start something and become distracted, you disqualify yourself from accomplishing Kingdom success. If you start the journey, you have to FINISH IT! It is actually better for you not to put your hands to the plow than to start the journey and quit.

Let me show you how serious this matter is. In Genesis 19, when Lot's family was leaving Sodom and Gomorrah, they were given very specific instructions to run for their lives and not look back. Everyone understood that they would be destroyed if they stopped or even looked back. Everyone followed the directions except Lot's wife. As a result of her looking back on the destruction that was taking place, she instantly turned into a pillar of salt. In this season, looking back would equate to crippling your financial freedom and entrepreneurial success. You have to decide that it is time for you to get busy birthing the dream that God has placed inside of you.

Let's look at Genesis 19:17. After they brought them out of the city, one of the men said, "Run for your lives! Don't look back or stop anywhere in the valley. Run to the mountains, or you will be destroyed" (New Century Version).

The instructions are clear. God is giving you the opportunity to leave the corrupt, ungodly culture that you are a part of and move into a place of purity and strength in life. If you are reading this book, you are ordained by God to be repositioned away from the things that were designed to destroy your spirit and hold you prisoner to unfulfillment. Your season of disgrace and destruction is over. Whatever you do, do not look back.

Dr. Cindy Trimm says that "last season's victory is this season's enemy." Lot's wife was so attached to yesterday that she could not mentally embrace what God wanted to do in her life today. Just like everyone on this journey, Lot's wife was afraid of the unknown. Evidently, her fear was stronger than her faith, and it caused her to miss what God had prepared for Lot's family. Do not allow the fear of the unknown to prevent you from seeing the complete manifestation of your vision.

You are reading this book because God wants to take you somewhere. Your faithfulness to Him has preserved your life while others perish. You survived the worst seasons of your life, now it is time for you to THRIVE. Your relationship is going to thrive. Your vision is going to manifest and prosper greatly.

We are living in a season where your actions speak louder than your words. As you begin the journey of reading this book, develop the mindset of a finisher. You cannot start this journey without the resolve to run all the way.

Not everyone who reads this book is in the same place. Metaphorically, our different places can be described like Elijah's journey during the drought in **I Kings 17**, *New International Reader's Version (NIRV)*.

2 Then a message came to Elijah from the Lord. He said, *3* "Leave this place. Go east and hide in the Kerith Valley. It is east of the Jordan River. *4* You will drink water from the brook. I have directed some ravens to supply you with food there." *5* So Elijah did what the Lord had told him to do. He went to the Kerith Valley. It was east of the Jordan River. He stayed there. *6* The ravens brought him bread and meat in the morning. They also brought him bread and meat in the evening. He drank water from the brook.

Some of you are reading the passage, and you are in the midst of a drought while waiting on instructions from the Lord. You may be laid off from a job because of downsizing, or you may have your job but have received a pay decrease because of corporate restructuring. In both of these situations, you are in a dry place waiting on instructions. Many of you may be like Elijah; you have commanded a drought based upon the words out of your mouth. What is unique about this text is the fact that Elijah declared a drought over the region in which he was dwelling, because of the corruption in that kingdom.

Next, the Lord speaks and tells Elijah that water will be available for him by the brook and that ravens will be supplying him with food. You may find yourself like Elijah. He has a water supply, but I never hear of the Lord's mentioning of any cups, or saucers, or dippers for Elijah to use to retrieve this water. So, he has water, but it stands to reason that he had to dip his hands down and drink out of his hands. Now, if you remember trying to do anything with water in your hands, you know that you really cannot get a lot to drink at a time when you are using your hands. It would stand to reason that his thirst was quieted but not silenced because he could never get the amount he needed all at one time. This to me sounds like all of us who live from paycheck to paycheck. You have just enough to keep the bill collectors away. You have just enough to keep the bills ahead of disconnection status, but you do not have enough to silence the thirst of financial freedom by paying those bills off or paying them off every month and having some money left over! Some of you may be in the next part of the story.

The second part of verse 4 says that the Lord has commanded some ravens to bring Elijah food. It is reasonable to believe that any time the Lord has to command someone to do something, it means that it is being done against that individual's will. Some of you are in situations in which you have employers who cannot stand you, but they cannot get rid of you. Something will not let them write that pink slip because of a skill the Lord caused that company to need that no one else can do except you. Therefore, you are there, but haters surround you. You are there, and you are getting the provision, but it is through the half-opened beak of a raven that does not like you at all, cannot stand to see you coming, but has instructions to leave you alone! Granted, this is not a great place to be in and that is okay because the story continues.

I Kings 17:7 (NIRV) says, "Sometime later the brook dried up." Therefore, even though those ravens had been bringing Elijah food in the morning and the evening, there was a new development. God interrupted the normal raven-feeding, brook-drinking drought fest with breaking news. God showed up to give Elijah his next stop on this journey. Here are the rest of the location stops on the Outrageous Dreamer Marathon.

1 Kings 17: 8-16 (NIV) states:

8 Then the word of the Lord came to him: **9** "Go at once to Zarephath in the region of Sidon and stay there. I have directed a widow there to supply you with food." **10** So he went to Zarephath. When he came to the town gate, a widow was there gathering sticks. He called to her and asked, "Would you bring me a little water in a jar so I may have a drink?" **11** As she was going to get it, he called, "And bring me, please, a piece of bread."

12 "As surely as the Lord your God lives," she replied, "I don't have any bread—only a handful of flour in a jar and a little olive oil in a jug. I am gathering a few sticks to take home and make a meal for myself and my son, that we may eat it—and die." **13** Elijah said to her, "Don't be afraid. Go home and do as you have said. But first make a small loaf of bread for me from what you have and bring it to me, and then make something for yourself and your son. **14** For this is what the Lord, the God of Israel, says: 'The jar of flour will not be used up and the jug of oil will not run dry until the day the Lord sends rain on the land.'" **15** She went away and did as Elijah had told her. So there was food every day for Elijah and for the woman and her family. **16** For the jar of flour was not used up and the jug of oil did not run dry, in keeping with the word of the Lord spoken by Elijah.

So, let us look at the journey:

1. Elijah had to move. He could not just stay in the location he was in and not heed the new directions. If he had not gone to the next place on the journey, he would have died because the water supply was gone. When you are in a place that is no longer taking care of your basic needs and God shows up with an "exit strategy," you do not have time to contend with God. You have to move!

2. Elijah had to ask someone he did not know for help. You might be at a place where you need some help, and the people that God places in your life may be new people. You cannot afford to let pride keep you from doing what the Lord tells you. The key to getting to the next leg of the Marathon is obedience in the current leg of the race. Obedience is key, no matter what side of the fence you find yourself. Keep in mind that the widow also had to exercise obedience when Elijah asked her to make him a cake.

3. You may be like the widow. She was ready and willing to get the prophet what he asked for based on what she could see. In verse 10, he asked for water; she had water. She could physically see it with her eyes; therefore, she went to get it without any hesitation. Things get a little tricky by verse 11. The prophet asks for a piece of bread. She now begins to describe to him the reason she cannot provide/share. Her reasons all stemmed from limitations in the natural. I am sure you have been there. Someone asks you to borrow some money. If you have it, then you might give it to the person, but if they say to you, "Hey, man, let me hold $200. By the time you lend it to me and I take care of my business, my paycheck will be in my account and I can give it right back to you." Now, if you are like most people, you may wonder, if the person has the ability to get what they need on their own "after" you have given them the money, what hindered them from taking care of their own need before you had to lend?

Well, in the natural, that thought process may seem reasonable, but in the Kingdom, God always requires a sacrifice for a better life. Life is better "after" the sacrifice. The greatest example of all time is the fact that all of our lives are better because of our Lord and Savior's death on the cross for our sins. Jesus, like the widow, asked if the cup could pass from Him. The widow is telling the prophet that she has to pass on his request because her natural eyes were looking at the ingredients in her possession.

4. An amazing turn of events took place as a result of her obedience. She was able to give the prophet the bread that he requested. She was able to feed her son and herself. Subsequently, the ingredients for making the bread did not run out and she was the only person in the area with the ability to produce bread. It sounds as if the Lord blessed her with her own business and made her instantly profitable.

That is the concept I want to impart into your life, your mind and your spirit. We have been sitting at the brook of corporate America. We have been given small amounts of money, just barely enough to get by, but God has another plan for His people that I can show to you by dissecting several translations of Jeremiah 29:11.

There are several scriptures in the Bible that we could use to explain the outpouring of anointing that is getting ready to overflow in your life and business. However, the one verse that the Lord has given to me is Jeremiah 29:11. If you look at this scripture, you may discover that every translation of it offers a little something different from the other.

Jeremiah 29:11, *New International Version (NIV)*
11 "For I know the plans I have for you," declares the Lord, "plans to prosper you and not to harm you, plans to give you hope and a future."

The NIV translation promises to "prosper you" and "not to harm you." Prosperity alone would have been a great gift to receive, but the Lord does not stop there. He then lets us know that we will not be harmed. Nothing is worse than owning something valuable and then not having insurance or a warranty on it. God gives us a guarantee that after we get our blessing, it will be safe. The verse ends by letting us know that God will give us hope and a future. I think it is important to note that in this verse, God gives us a hope and a future. Hope means "elpis". "Elpis" simply means the expectation of good. Some scholars further translate "elpis" to mean confident expectation. This is important because even when you are blessed and protected, you will begin believing for the next thing. You will believe for more, bigger and greater. God is letting you know that no matter what it looks like, you can stop worrying and stressing because you have an expectation of good for your future.

Jeremiah 29:11, *New Life Version (NLV).*
11 "For I know the plans I have for you,'" says the Lord, "plans for well-being and not for trouble, to give you a future and a hope.'"

The NLV translation promises us that God plans well-being for our lives, not trouble. I believe this Word is profound because it is possible to live a life of well-being when you properly place your life in the Master's hands. I am not saying that you never face trouble, but when you do face it, this verse assures that God is going to give you a future and a hope. This translation switches the words future and hope. I believe that switch is made because even when your future gets here, you have to have a confident expectation that calamity is not around the corner. In addition, this verse helps us know that once our future arrives, we can have the expectation of the God we serve to protect our possessions so that we are not constantly stressed out all the time. We can cast our cares on Him, for He cares for us. The Lord stands ready to take the load, but we just have to be ready to release it and turn it over to Him.

Jeremiah 29:11, *New American Standard Bible (NASB).*
11 "For I know the plans that I have for you,'" declares the Lord, "'plans for welfare and not for calamity to give you a future and a hope.'"

The NASB keeps future and hope in the same order, but it says that God knows the plans He has for us, "plans for welfare and not for calamity."

Now, I know that here in America, welfare has a bit of a negative connotation to it, but if you look up its definition, you will get a new revelation.

It gives readers two sets of words to describe it:

1. health, comfort, security, safety, protection, prosperity, success, fortune; interest, good.

2. social security, social assistance, benefit, public assistance; pension, credit, support; sick pay, unemployment benefit

Nineteen words are listed in this definition. Notice that while you are on your way to the future that He has planned for you, God has backup plans within the backup plan to get you to a prosperous place. Did you notice that public assistance is in the mix and that sick pay and unemployment benefits are listed? That says to me that if I get sick, the Lord has a plan. Then, if I lose my job, while I am on my way to becoming an outrageous dreamer, He has an unemployment benefit already waiting for me! The thing I want you to see is that the translator uses one word that can have almost 20 power-packed words in them while rebuking calamity. Therefore, no crisis, no challenge, no difficulty, no utter devastation, or destruction is going to be able to take root in your life because you have a future and a hope!

Now I hope all of that blessed you, but I am not done. I have one more point, and I really saved the best for last.

Jeremiah 29:11 *(The Message Bible).*
"I know what I'm doing. I have it all planned out—plans to take care of you, not abandon you, plans to give you the future you hope for."

Now, I want you to read this verse in the Message translation three times. Go ahead. After you take a victory lap around your office, house, Starbucks, or wherever you may be, look at it one more time with me.

1. God says, "'I know what I am doing.'" I am not sure if you have ever been in a situation where someone was doing something for you that seemed like it was way more of a punishment than a present. I do not know if you have ever started working out with a physical trainer. Some of the things that the trainer will have you

do may not really make any sense to you. For example, someone tells a trainer that he or she wants to lose weight in his or her waist and obtain abs. You would think that the trainer would put the person on the Ab row machine; the Ab ripper machine; the Ab track; and the Ab cycle, but that is not what happens at all. The trainer tells you that you need a trio of specific diet, weight training and cardio to get the desired results. Now, if you are like me, those three things may not seem to you like the regimen that would help anyone get abs. I learned something though--the trainer knows what he or she is doing. If you follow his or her lead, you will get just what you want. It is the same way with God. If you just sit back and wait on the Lord, and be of good courage, you will see the goodness of the Lord in the land of the living.

2. In the next sentence, God says, "I have it all planned out." 1 Corinthians 2:9 (NKJV) reads: But as it is written:
    "Eye has not seen, nor ear heard,

    Nor have entered into the heart of man

    The things which God has prepared for those who love Him."

    Not only does God have a plan for you, it is so big that it cannot be conceptualized in the natural mind. The plans are so incredible that they cannot adequately be perceived in the human mind. The plans are so amazing, you just have to sit patiently and receive it. If that does not excite you, the next part will!

3. The last section has a 3-part blessing.

    A. He promises to take care of you.
    B. He promises never to abandon you.
    C. He has plans to give you "the future you hope for."

So, if God is going to take care of you, He is going to bless you—pressed down, shaken together and running over. If He has promised never to abandon you, even if your mother and father forsake you, He has promised to be there with you until the end. Finally, the part that really sets my soul on fire comes: He is going to give you what you hope for! This means not only does God have a plan for you; it is a future you will be happy about. It is the future of your dreams aligned with his perfect plan for you. I hope you are excited about that, because I am excited for you. The first day of your life as an "Outrageous Dreamer" begins today.

At the end of every section, I am going to give you some assignments. Before you begin reading chapter one, get a journal or special notebook and complete your assignments there. Do not cheat yourself by ignoring this step. It is an essential component to birthing your dream.

CHAPTER 2

IT'S TIME TO LIVE THE LIFE OF YOUR DREAMS

The first reason to step into and pursue your dream is obvious—you want to fulfill your purpose and tap into the prosperous life that you desire. That is great. It really is, but I want to let you know you should be pursuing your dream for another reason: to live the life you dream about repeatedly. It is time to bring it to reality.

This morning, I woke up singing one of my favorite songs "This is your life." When I think about the lyrics of this popular composition by Switchfoot, I am challenged to reevaluate the quality of my life. The lyrics of this song ring in my mind this morning. "This is your life, are you who you want to be? This is your life is it everything you dreamed it would be?"

This morning, I began by asking myself the question, what is hindering me from living the life of my dreams? This allowed me to find key distractions in my life and character that block my success. I developed a list of five things that we must be determined to stop today from hindering our success.

1. Stop living life without a plan. This is such a critical part of living the life of your dreams. Before you can live the life of your dreams, you must first have a dream. Take time to develop a plan for every day of your life and watch how things change.

2. Stop giving yourself excuses. "Excuses are alibis for poverty and failure." What else is there to say? Do not allow your excuses to control of your life any longer. You can carry out whatever you wish. NO MORE EXCUSES!

3. Stop giving people and situations the power to control your environment. Anybody who can control your mood or attitude has power over you. They almost have complete dominion over your life. Find them and take back your personal power.

4. Stop working harder on someone else's dream than you do on your own. Unfortunately, we have been wired to ensure the success of others and never our own success. This is unfortunate because we will put all of our time and energy into other people, but allow our vision to die. Rewire your mind and make a decision to see your dreams live.

5. Stop living someone else's dream for you and live the life of your dreams. There are so many people in the world who live unfulfilled lives because they are living the life someone else created for them. This is your life.

Are you who you want to be? Is this the life that you dreamed of or the life someone else dreamed for you? Take charge of your life and live it for you today.

Let us make the right change today!

OUTRAGEOUS ACTIVITIES:

1. *Write the vision and make it plain.*

2. *List people who hinder you from fulfilling your dream.*

3. *List the circumstances that hinder you from pursuing your dream.*

4. *List people who encourage you to fulfill your dream.*

5. *Pray for the strength to begin eliminating the hindering people and circumstances from your life.*

CHAPTER 3

LET'S EVALUATE SO WE CAN ELEVATE

efore we can truly get you on the path to pursuing your vision, we must first evaluate where you are in life. Your accomplishments or accolades do not measure true success. I have learned that happiness is the measure of true success. True success is fulfillment.

I had a life that looked good but did feel good. Externally, you would have thought that everything was perfect, but internally things felt horrible.

If you are currently feeling some kind of way about life right now, here are three reasons why:

1. **You are living outside of your purpose**—If you have read my book, Outrageous Vision, you know that one of my favorite quotes is "Purpose is the seat of fulfillment. If what you are doing is not fulfilling you, then you might be living outside of purpose."

When you are not living a purpose-driven life, you are heading down the road to destruction. You become a victim of unhappiness and ultimately depression. Take a moment and evaluate the areas in your life where you feel unfulfilled. Do you feel called to that area? Does the passion still exist?

2. **You have outgrown your current situation—**You have exhausted your current level. Occasionally I will play video games on my iPhone. Do not judge me! I have been playing this game called "Hay Day" for about 6 months. At first, things were cool because I felt like I was making progress. I was logging in every chance I could get. Six months later, I might log in in every few days. The thrill is gone!

Why, because it no longer seems profitable. Every time I log in it seems like the same old thing. It is no longer fulfilling its purpose because I have tapped out. There was a level of enjoyment at the beginning that no longer exists.

If this sounds like your life, then it is time to do something different. The less profitable you feel in life, the more irritated you are with life. Grow to the next level.

3. **You live life based on the roles you play, not based upon your passion—**One thing I have learned is that the ultimate key to a purposeful life is a passion-filled life.

Your purpose is directly connected to the things that you are most passionate about. My passion is to see people happy and prosperous, so I enjoy spending time coaching people who are ready to take their life to the next level.

Another passion of mine is music! I sing all of the time. I sing so much that people tell me to shut up! It is very fulfilling for me to travel and perform in front of thousands of people. What are you passionate about? Your passion is the most critical part of your purpose. It is essential that your vision and your dream are connected to it.

Let us be clear. You cannot be a successful business owner just by creating a product or offering a service. You have to infuse your passionate, authentic interest and insight to whatever package you are offering to the public. In a world of copies, you must pursue being an original at all costs. Your passions will not only help you plan your path to becoming an outrageous dreamer, but they also guarantee your success at whatever business you create.

So, let us recap. No matter how you feel about your current life, through the next series of days and nights of reading this book, your life is going to go to another level. If you have evaluated your life as POOR or FAIR—you are only going up from here. If your life is good, then you are closer to achieving that OUTRAGEOUS status.

The key is identifying where you are and preparing to go to the next level. The next level will require you actively attaching your passion to every area of your life.

OUTRAGEOUS ACTIVITIES:

1. *Where did you rate your life?*

   POOR | FAIR | GOOD

2. *What are you passionate about? (What would you do almost for free because you love it so much?)*

3. *How will you incorporate your passion into your dream/vision/business?*

CHAPTER 4

EMBRACING AND EMBALMING THE "REAL YOU"

Now I know that chapter title seems extreme. One of the biggest obstacles to obtaining the success that we seek is not really understanding or liking who you are.

Do you like who you are or do you feel a deep and enduring need to change?

Maybe you feel a little of both. With that being said, some things you need to embrace about yourself, and some things you need to embalm. Some things just have no place in your life if you are going to advance to the next level and manifest your dream. Most of us, at some point in our lives, feel a desire to change some aspect of ourselves. We do not like how we look, or we worry that some deep-seated personality trait, such as a fiery temper or jealousy, will negatively affect our relationships with other people.

Where does the pressure to change come from? Is it the result of a positive attitude, an internal drive to improve ourselves? Alternatively, is it reactive, a response to something external? Does the distinction even matter?

Change is a Choice

Every change, whether it is the hairstyle you wear or a major life decision, such as where to live or whether to start a family, involves a choice. Other people might try to influence your decision, but you are the only one who can make it. You do this by considering the merits of the options in front of you, and voluntarily choosing to perform one of the options because it offers better rewards or ethically is the right thing to do. You may choose to do nothing at all.

What I would like to point out is that we rarely choose to change for its own sake. We seek to change ourselves because we care for one another, and ourselves. We appreciate that other people have an essential place in our lives, and we want to do our best by them. We feel this intrinsically, deep in our hearts. Occasionally, we receive a push or a criticism from someone else, which reminds us that we are not the best person we could be.

Changing ourselves is a selfless act. And by that, I mean that changing yourself demands going out of your way to help others--to eradicate the things that cause negative energy in your relationships and bring positive energies to others.

Changing yourself does not involve changing who you are. When someone calls you an idiot, they rarely mean that you are an idiot; they mean that you have acted without thinking, or spoken without considering the consequences of your words. They are not criticizing who they are. They are criticizing how you are—how you handle situations, and what you do.

You already have the capacity to be cheerful, loving, gracious, empathic, ambitious, influential and kind. Everyone does. However, you may need help bringing out those positive characteristics. You may need to change the way you do things so that your actions align with your psyche. This is not changing who you are. It is synergizing your personality and your choices, to reveal a more authentic you.

COMPLETE THIS OUTRAGEOUS CHALLENGE:

For one day, consciously choose to act in a way that reveals the very best you. In your interactions with other people, choose to be tolerant, choose to be resilient, and choose to be kind.

Forewarning: This exercise is hard. It demands introspection. It demands that you look within your mind and observe yourself thinking. Before you can make the right decision, you will need to figure out why you sometimes make the wrong decision—what propensities, habits and motivations trigger certain emotions or cause you to act against your own best interests.

If by the end of the day, you have made authentic choices when in the past you did not, you will realize that you can change, and have changed. You will know who you are, and you can start using your thinking, speaking and actions to create more happiness, success and fulfillment. I know you can do it! Once you have completed the challenge, come back and answer the questions below in your journal or special notebook:

OUTRAGEOUS ACTIVITY:

1. ***After doing the exercise above, what revelations have you had about yourself?***

2. ***What revelations have you had about others?***

3. ***What characteristics about yourself do you feel you need to change to be successful?***

4. ***What attributes do you already have that will contribute to your success?***

5. ***How can you enhance or develop the positive attributes you already have?***

CHAPTER 5

DEFINE HAPPINESS FOR YOURSELF (Even If It is Not What People Expect)

Do you feel tethered? Tethered to your job, your home, your debt, your gadgets, and your shoe fetish? Tethered to the same old you every day, the one that is busy in a whirlwind of activity but ultimately going nowhere? Just like a hamster on a wheel, your life is not going to change direction unless you start doing things differently.

Most of us play safe. Consciously or not, we urge caution, hunker down, and evade pain. We grow up dreaming of being astronauts and ballerinas. We dream beyond the limits of the possible.

On the contrary, the life of an "outrageous dreamer" often requires choosing the "road less traveled." At some point along the way, we reject the notion that the life of commuting and cubicles is one we want to live. However, if we are not careful and we do not listen to our hearts, we make a decision to endure quietly the things that make us unhappy in the slow suffocation of the comfort zone.

The reason? We are terrified of falling short. None of us is perfect, yet we set cruelly high bars for ourselves. We

worry that stepping out of the comfort zone—changing direction and taking risks—will set us up to fail. So, we carry on doing the same old same old, just to show that we are good enough, even if it does not make us happy.

One of the problems is that many people listen to outside advice rather than following their inner voice. They treat as gospel a laundry list of "shoulds"—should go to college, should be married by 30, should stay in a decent but ill-fitting job. Should is a dangerous word. It sets up a real dissonance between what others expect of you and the things that truly make your heart shine.

There is absolutely nothing in this life that you "should" do. The route to happiness is not fixed, but rather a series of forks in the road. Like Frost, you might take the one less traveled by or you may take the popular path. It does not matter, as long as you follow your heart at every turn. Do that and you will arrive at a happy place.

Guess what—it is a different place for everyone. Would you like to know the real secret to happiness?

The reason why some people find fulfillment, abundance and love is simple—they believe their happiness is important. They give themselves permission to be happy on their own terms. At the risk of sounding like an L'Oréal ad, they think they are worth it. Happy people truly feel worthy of happiness. They make choices that reinforce their happiness, and they pursue those choices whole-heartedly. They do not make excuses. When someone asks them why they have not bought a house yet, they joyfully answer, "because right now I would rather start my own business/commune with nature/take time to be a mom."

You deserve to face each day with something more than quiet resignation. You deserve to love your job, your relationships, and your journey. You deserve to feel that your dreams count, because they do. Accept that happiness is a necessity. Give yourself permission to want the things you know can make you happy and then figure out how to get them.

Here are a few nuggets of knowledge that will help you on your way:

» *Make happiness a standard by which to measure your choices. Any decision that frustrates your happiness is a poor one.*

» *Consciously invest in your happiness. This takes time and effort, but once you start exercising that muscle, it will get easier.*

» *Be as kind to yourself as you are to others.*

» **_Assume you will be just fine when you take a risk - you likely will be._**

» **_Learn to ask for help when you need it._**

» **_Embrace the great things that happen in your life, no matter how small. These things do not happen by chance. They happen because you deserve them._**

» **_Who you are is enough. In fact, who you are is MORE than enough. Repeat as often as necessary. Smile broadly._**

The reason it is so imperative that you embrace a new set of rules for happiness is that you are preparing yourself for a completely different life than most people choose. Most people play it safe because they believe that is the only way to ensure happiness when actually it rarely works out for most people. Think about it. Most people work for 40-50 years at a series of jobs that they do not like only to retire on 40 percent of their income (if they are lucky). The catch is that people retire and are trying to live on less income than they were making when they were working. Then they get a part-time job or worse, they cannot retire at all. That is not the future of an outrageous dreamer. Our futures require being happy to take the risk to secure a future that most of our peers cannot imagine. Adjust your present definition of happiness to secure an almost unmeasurable, undefinable level of happiness for your future.

OUTRAGEOUS ACTIVITY:

1. *What is your definition of happiness after reading this chapter?*

2. *What is your plan to pursue your dream (based on this chapter) to obtain it?*

3. *What are positive affirmations that you can create (based on this chapter) to encourage you while you are pursuing your dream?*

CHAPTER 6

IDENTITY CHECK (Are You Your Worse Enemy?)

Are you unlucky in love? Continually passed over for promotion or used by colleagues? When these things happen, you might joke about how unlucky you are or how God has it in for you. The chances are YOU are to blame. The culprit is a nasty little demon called self-sabotage.

Self-sabotage is a survival mechanism. It kicks into action when you are scared about the outcome of a situation, so you avoid that situation to protect yourself from getting hurt. Like a devil sitting on your shoulder, self-sabotage is your voice shouting that you are just not loveable, or you are not cut out for a demanding new business, so there is no point in trying. This is one of the most important chapters in this book. So many people gain success only to lose it because of the "man in the mirror."

If you just cannot figure out why you are not as successful as you should be, one of these culprits might be to blame:

1. **You believe you are not good enough**—A massive 70% of lottery winners end up living paycheck to paycheck within just seven years of their big win. Why? Because they feel like imposters. They have not earned the money, so they do not think they deserve it. You may believe that the people around you are successful because they are better than you in some way—more intelligent, more capable or more likeable. No matter what you are planning to do, you assume that your efforts will fail because you lack the essential ingredients for success. So, what do you do? You let your poor self-image hold you hostage. You panic and throw in the towel at the first hurdle. Unsurprisingly, the results you produce—if you produce any at all—suck.

Now when you judge your performance, you can legitimately say that you have failed. At this point, you feel even more insecure, disillusioned and deflated. Like those lottery winners, you think that you are unworthy of success, so you put off looking for the job or relationship you really want because you believe you are a failure.

If this is you, **STOP**! Stop thinking about self-worth in terms of the outcome of your actions, and start measuring the effort you put into them. Learn to be kind to yourself. Once you start being compassionate towards your own accomplishments you will realize that you do, in fact, have what it takes to succeed. Take it from me; everyone has the power to be extraordinary. You just need to dream it and do it.

2. **You try to please everyone**—Friend, are you running yourself ragged looking after children, compulsively over-committing to the needs of your managers and colleagues, cleaning the house, organizing family and work activities—all while silently seething at the injustice of it all? If so, you are a people-pleaser.

   As a people-pleaser, you think you are doing good deeds. However, what you are really doing is giving other people way too much power over your destiny. Instead of shaping your life from the inside out, you are letting other people shape your life from the outside in. When this happens, you lose sight of your passion. Worse, you build up massive stores of bitterness towards the people who you blame for standing in the way of your dreams. If those people sense your lingering resentment—and they usually do—they will not trust you and your work prospects and relationships will suffer. I firmly believe that we are all standing on the brink of great victories in our lives. By learning how to articulate your own thoughts and needs, you can create a passion-filled life that is still respectful of the people you care about.

3. **You sweep problems under the rug**—Denial is a particular type of defense mechanism that helps us avoid potentially distressing situations. By refusing to believe a problem exists, we do not feel bad about the problem. Of course, while you are busy sticking your head in the sand, the problem is still there, gnawing away at you and jeopardizing your chances of success.

The thing about problems is they rarely go away on their own. Left unattended, they grow and escalate until they become too big to handle by ordinary methods. One example is the man who puts off visiting the doctor when he finds a lump because he is afraid of what the doctor will find. By the time he builds up the courage to ask for help, the lump can no longer be treated with drugs and requires major surgery to remove it.

Denial is harmful. It stops us from questioning our role in dilemmas and paying attention to the negative themes that recur in our lives. Next time you are late for a meeting, stop and think why. Have you convinced yourself that your tardiness does not matter? Have you resolved that everyone is late these days? If so, you are denying the truth—that you are disrespecting your colleagues' time and dishonoring your working relationships.

If you find yourself in the same situation, failing repeatedly, you are probably in denial about something. It is time to engage in some soul-searching to break the cycle.

4. **You are a perfectionist—**To the outside world, the perfectionist seems confident, intelligent and self-aware when, in actuality, on the inside she is suffering. She is suffering because she has set unrealistic standards for herself and never seems to achieve the "perfect" way of living she thinks should attain.

Perfection is like an endless ladder stretching up into the sky. When you strive for perfection, you always fail, because there is always another rung to climb that will take you to dizzier heights. Been promoted to manager? Great! But the perfectionist wants to be CEO. Promoted to CEO? Amazing! But, to the perfectionist, there is always a bigger company, a more reputable industry or a friend who is even more successful at the top. Perfectionists fail because there is no level of attainment at which they will not fail. The concept is an imperfect paradigm. You must overcome this now because when you are running your own business, it will make you abandon it to do something that seems bigger or better, but may not be connected to your gifting or passion. Everything you do must be connected to your passion for you to be successful, but self-sabotage will trick you if you are not careful!

Perfectionism is a form of bondage. It manacles you in misery because nothing you do will ever live up to your high expectations. Flexibly striving for good enough results rather than rigidly looking for perfection can make all the difference. That way, you will take pride in your successes and learn to enjoy the pure pleasure of performing a task rather than being hung up on an ideal outcome.

Self-sabotage is a sneaky demon. Harness your courage, embrace it and put a stop to it!

OUTRAGEOUS ACTIVITIES:

1. *Are you a current victim of self-sabotage?*

2. *If yes, which of the above four areas do you struggle with?*

3. *If no, which area is most likely to try to attack you?*

4. *How will you prevent and break free from the bondage of self-sabotage?*

CHAPTER 7

FEAR PART ONE:

The Great Failure Hoax: Is Fear Standing in the Way of Your Success?

"Never confuse a single defeat with a final defeat"
- F. Scott Fitzgerald

Have you ever put off doing something because you are scared of how it might turn out? If so, you are not alone. So many of us are afraid of failing, the neurosis has its own medical diagnosis (it is **atychiphobia**, the irrational fear of failing, in case you are interested!)

The thing is, it is almost impossible to go through life without experiencing some level of failure. Most of us fail at the micro-level every day. We forget to pass on messages, miss deadlines or prepare poorly for class. These are mechanical failures, so routine we hardly notice them. But on a subconscious level, these failures hurt us. They fill us to the brim with unpleasant feelings such as disappointment, frustration, regret and anger. They make us feel bad about who we are as people. They make us feel shame, and shame is toxic. It is associated with something I call the "Doomsday" paradigm of failure. People with a "Doomsday mindset" see failure as the end of the world. When they fail, to whatever degree, they think they are incompetent, or inadequate, or do not deserve the opportunities that come their way. Heck, their failure is proof that they are these things. To coin a common phrase, failure is not something they do, it is something they are. That "something" drastically lowers their chances of success.

Successful people do not associate "failure" with "shame."

Do you think that entrepreneurs, superstar celebrities, high- performance athletes and self-made millionaires only experience victories on their road to the top? Of course not! For every victory, there is usually a colossal failure or two.

For example:

» ***Oprah Winfrey was fired from her first job in TV before rising to become the "Queen of all Media," the richest African-American of the 20th Century and one of Time magazine's most influential people.***

» ***Steven Spielberg, winner of three Academy Awards for Best Director, was rejected by the University of Southern California's School of Cinematic Arts not once but THREE times.***

» ***JK Rowling, the world's first billionaire author, was a broke single mom when she penned the first book in the Harry Potter series. Twelve publishers famously rejected her book before Bloomsbury picked it up—after the Chairman's eight-year-old daughter begged her father to print it.***

Here is the thing: successful people do not think "Doomsday." When they fail, they pick themselves up, brush themselves off and figure out a way to do it better next time. Steven Spielberg did not let a "C" grade in a television production course hold him back. No Sir. He took it as a sign that he was not cut out for school and dropped out to pursue his passion. He overlooked the minor battle-defeat to focus on the war.

The interesting thing is, the more successful people fail, the better they get at success. This happens for two reasons. First, they believe that victory is possible so they never stop pursuing their goals. Second, when success finally comes their way, they do not reject it as people with the "Doomsday" mindset might. They believe they have earned their success through guts, struggle and perseverance—and that allows them to embrace their victory with open arms.

Let me tell you, success is possible! You just have to have faith in yourself and see failure for the incredible learning opportunity it really is. When every project we attempt has two possible outcomes, success or failure, the law of averages tells us that we will experience failure 50% of the time. Facing that chance demands courage—but it will give you a richer, more rewarding life.

So, no matter what fear has tried to hold you hostage, today I am speaking against that and adding my faith to yours for your business and dream. You are on your way to a rewarding and amazing life. Believe with me for your future today! I am cheering for you all the way!

OUTRAGEOUS ACTIVITY:

1. **Write down all the possible outcomes of a decision.** *In some cases, the worst-case scenario will genuinely be disastrous and justify your fear of failure. However, most of the time you will see at a glance all the good things that could happen if you just have the courage to move forward.*

2. **Write down your contingency plan.** *Get yourself a low-risk backup plan. (This can help you feel more comfortable about taking a calculated risk).*

3. **Write down a list of people who can help you and ask for help.** *Positive people are your secret weapon. They can help you keep your eyes on the prize when you are paralyzed by fear.*

CHAPTER 8

FEAR PART TWO:

Overcome Fear-Take the First Step

Fear, not the lack of good ideas, "keeps a person standing on the sideline."
–Andy Stanley

In Chapter 7, we began to talk about fear. It is critical that you conquer it because it is one of the greatest enemies of vision is fear. You know fear—that feeling of discomfort that shows up every time you are getting ready to make a major move in your life. It is an unpleasant, often strong emotion caused by anticipation or awareness of danger. This emotion can make or break you. It has the power to fuel your dreams or destroy them.

I believe fear was never designed to stop us completely from chasing new opportunities. It was created as a tool to help us move into new opportunities with caution and count up all the costs before making the big steps. In most cases, we allow fear to hinder us from moving forward by becoming overly cautious and afraid.

Most people will tell you that the first step is always the hardest step to take. I honestly believe it is the hardest step because we spend time over calculating every situation. The first step is what counts. Look at what Andy Stanley says about fear:

If you are tired of being on the sidelines and you are ready to take action, then you are in the right place. The fear of moving forward can be destroyed by taking several steps.

The first step is the most difficult to take.

Take a look at a few things you can do to fight the fear of moving forward:

1. **Take the First Step! Vision is initiated by taking calculable first steps—**Dreams die because the dreamer is afraid of taking this first step of deciding to pursue it. There is nothing to it but to do it.

2. **Do Not Allow Fear to Overpower Your Faith—**Your dreams must be more powerful than your fears. Faith and fear are incompatible. They cannot exist in the same mental or physical context. You have to believe that this can happen more than you doubt.

3. **Ignore the Voice of Negativity. Your faith comes by what you hear—**What you hear will always decide what you can carry out. Ultimately, whom you hear controls your future. Surround your life with faith-filled

people who speak positively into your future. Their words will help you do anything.

4. **Fight Fear with Courage. Courage is the weapon needed to fight fear**—Courage is essential to the success of your dream. It takes courage to carry out your vision. Courage means to have the mental or moral strength to venture, persevere, and withstand danger, fear, or difficulties. It is having the mental stability needed to complete your assigned task.

5. **Celebrate Failures as Learning Experiences**—No matter how well you plan or dream; you will meet failure at several points in your journey. Nobody starts our perfect. Every attempt takes you closer and closer to perfection. Do not become defeated in moments of failure; learn from them.

As you are on your journey to accomplishing greatness, learn how to use fear as a navigational tool. Let it help you make the right decisions instead of hinder you from accomplishing good success.

OUTRAGEOUS ACTIVITIES:

1. *What is one thing you can do to take the first step to overcome the fears that you listed in the previous chapter?*

2. *Whom can you ask to be an accountability partner with you to keep you from procrastinating?*

54

3. *When will you do it? Give yourself a deadline and ask your accountability partner to help you.*

CHAPTER 9

LIVE COURAGEOUSLY

Some of the people we admire the most are those who suffered with insurmountable loss or pain but maintained an attitude of positivity, gratitude, and dignity. Stuart Scott, beloved ESPN anchor, is one of those respected individuals. He is remembered for so many amazing things, but one of them was his ability to still be devoted to his craft and his daughters in the midst of a courageous fight against cancer.

In his 2014 Espy acceptance speech, Scott said something about his fight with cancer that literally changed my perspective on life. Scott said:

"When you die, it does not mean that you lose to cancer. You beat cancer by how you live, why you live, and in the manner in which you live."

This amazing quote proves that Stuart Scott lived a courageous, victorious, optimistic life despite the adversity he had to face every day. His victory was not a product of a surgery or being healed from his condition. His victory was a product of his positive mindset. Scott looked at life through the lens of vision and refused to allow the negatives in his life to control his future. We must be this same way. We have all heard the phrase, "When life gives you lemons, make lemonade." Well, for most people, that is much easier said than done.

Looking at your life with an optimistic attitude will allow you to maintain a positive mindset. You have to learn how to celebrate life's ups and downs and treat them as opportunities for greatness. Learn how to see some good in everything that happens in your life.

For this to take place, a paradigm shift is required. A paradigm is a worldview. It is your broad, but finite perception of what is happening in the world around you or to you. Your perception is ultimately your reality. The only way you can change your reality is by changing the way you think.

Going through any type of challenge or trial will bring depression and discontentment if you only focus on the negative of the situation.

I believe there are three things that you can do to ensure that you maintain positive thinking in a negative situation.

1. **Maintain an attitude of gratitude**—Grateful people are normally the happiest people on the planet. They know how to find something to be grateful for in every situation, i.e. realizing that things could be worst or that someone else did not live through what you grew through.

2. **Be happy in your faith!**—The enemy of fear is faith. I believe that faith is the most powerful force in the universe. Faith has the power to guide you through the roughest situations of your life. Find something good to believe in and hold fast to the profession of your faith without wavering or doubting.

3. **Focus on the good**—Do not allow your feelings or emotions make you feel less satisfied than you really are. When you shift your focus on the better things in life, you will find yourself making history. Focusing on the good causes you to become unstoppable.

OUTRAGEOUS ACTIVITY:

1. *What is the one situation that was tough for you, but living through it changed your life for the better?*

2. *What are three things that you are believing for this year?*

    A. _______________________________

    B. _______________________________

    C. _______________________________

3. *Who is one person that is an ultimate optimist in your life? A person that always sees the positive in every situation. What lessons can you learn or have you learned from him or hear?*

CHAPTER 10

SURVIVING SEASONS OF CHANGE

Change can be one of the most difficult experiences we have to face in life. We experience change in so many areas of life, from the food we eat to the clothes we buy. Change is a major part of our world.

I do not know about where you live but here in Atlanta, Georgia, today is an extremely cold day. It is crazy because yesterday was extremely warm. It feels like the temperature has shifted from summer to winter overnight.

Living in weather like this, it is hard to discern the season. I mean, one day it is hot enough for flip-flops and today it is just about cold enough to wear long johns.

That is how life is. Sometimes things can shift drastically overnight and you can become confused about which season you are living in. For most people, one moment they are enjoying the joys of summer and the next they are trying to endure the massive storms of the winter.

In every area of life, change can happen at a rapid pace. Your career, relationship, assignment, all can shift at a moment's notice. The best thing you can do is be ready to handle seasons of change.

I have learned a few things that I believe will equip you to handle change better when you experience it:

1. **Understand that change is an agent of growth—** Every season has an assignment to play in growing you to the next level of success. Look at it as change being hired by growth to get you to the next level.

2. **When your season changes, you automatically change—**You require different things in different seasons. You do not wear a bikini in the winter to a ski resort. Do not get stuck trying to keep the things from last season in this season. Identify the tools and connections you need to complete your assignment in this season.

3. **Understand the power of your season—**Instead of complaining about what is wrong, discover your assignment for that season of your life. There is an assignment that you must complete in every season to be successful. Your power is connected to your assignments. Ants work in the summer so that they can survive in the wintertime.

4. **Educate yourself on the skills needed to survive your current season and prepare for your next season—**Knowledge is power! Not only is it power, but also it is empowerment. Most people panic in seasons

of change because they do not have knowledge or understanding. Strategy is everything. Get wisdom and in all of your getting, get an understanding.

5. **Last Season's victory is this season's enemy**—When change hits our lives, we often try to reach for what worked for us in our past. Life does not always work like that. Embrace fresh strategies so you can produce better results in your new season.

6. **Do not allow yesterday to hold you hostage**—Most people go through life living in a new place with an old mentality. If you change your thoughts, you can change your life. Embrace a new day so that you can see glorious victories.

OUTRAGEOUS ACTIVITY:

1. *Recall an instance where there was an abrupt change in your life. How did you handle the change in "season?" How did you grow because of it?*

2. *Identify three tools you feel are necessary to be successful in this season of your life.*

3. *Are there any old strategies/approaches being used that are proving ineffective in this season? What new strategies are you willing to implement?*

CHAPTER 11

YOUR JOURNEY IS WHAT YOU MAKE IT

Life is a journey! Everybody's journey is different and filled with obstacles. At the end of the day, your journey is what you make it.

Recently, I was introduced to the amazing journey of NYT Best Selling author, Kris Carr. Back in 2003, Kris was diagnosed with a rare and incurable stage four cancer. After receiving this tragic news, Kris had a decision to make and she definitely made the right decision. Kris said that this defining moment caused her to upgrade her life inside and out. Even though she would live life with a disease that could not be cured, she could take charge of her health and live her best life.

Kris's testimony was so remarkable that she was featured on Oprah Winfrey's Super Soul Sunday. As she shared her story, there were three principles that really grabbed my attention. I think they will empower you.

Here are the Principles:

Principle 1: While all great life lessons give us opportunities, they are sometimes masked as obstacles.

Life is an obstacle course with many different opportunities for you to win. When you are learning, you are never losing. Why? Because knowledge is a critical part of success. Learn how to view every obstacle, whether good or bad, as an opportunity to take your life to the next level.

Principle 2: Do not waste your life waiting for joy and realize that joy is all around you.

Most people go through life looking for reasons to celebrate, not realizing that the opportunity to live in this time is the greatest reason to be happy. Discover the small things in life, and learn how to celebrate them. Realize that there is always something to be grateful for and happy about.

Principle 3: We are all going to die but how many of us will truly live?

Out of everything Kris Carr said during her recent interview, this final principle stuck out the most to me. Life is a gift that God gives us every day. The life that we receive will end at some point. Learn how to maximize the gift that you have been given and live life every day.

OUTRAGEOUS ACTIVITY:

1. *What is one obstacle that you are currently facing that after reading this chapter you now see it as an opportunity? List it here.*

2. *List five things/people that you are grateful for?*

CHAPTER 12

THE POWER OF CONVERSATION

Do you know that every idea has an audience? I live by this belief. You should too. When God gives you something—an idea, a passion, or a mission—you are not the only recipient. God wants you to share your gift with the world. You are responsible for developing the strategies to take your idea or your message to the world. Of course, "the world" has a variety of meanings.

You cannot reach everybody. Even if you could, not everyone would accept or support your message. Show me the world's most popular author/speaker, and I will show you hundreds, if not thousands, who disagree with his ideology, his communication style, or even the way he lives his personal life. Want proof? Choose any best-selling book and look up all the reviews on a major website like Amazon.com. Read the most negative reviews and note how vicious they can be.

As I write this chapter, Bill O'Reilly's book Legends and Lies: The Real West is a best-seller, with scores of rave reviews. However, it has garnered several one-star reviews (on a five-star scale) on Amazon. One reviewer calls the book "Another fraud book by a fraud." Another says, "Bill... you really blew it!"

I will say it again: No one was meant to serve everybody. Nobody, even a best-selling author, can please all the people all of the time.

A few years ago, I wrote a blog titled "The Power of Conversation." I stated that every idea has an audience; however, as visionaries, we have to find the right audience to share our ideas with. A conversation is only powerful when it is shared with the right audience. As my ministry has grown over the past few years, I believe now more than ever that we all have ideas that need to be shared with our worlds. Every idea has people it will affect. Your ideas matter and your life can take on new meaning when you believe that you have something to offer your world.

I promise you this: There are people out there who want to hear what you have to say.

I know that last sentence might be hard for you to believe, especially in a world filled with critics. When you see all of the negativity expressed on social media, for example, it is easy to doubt yourself. It is easy to think, "People will criticize my ideas" or "I don't know if my ideas have a place in society."

One way to get past this self-doubt is to realize that you do not have to share your ideas with the entire world.

The blog you write, the book you author, the speech you give does not have to be accepted by everybody in order for you to be successful. Some authors write a book and then hope it meets the approval of every person on the planet. That is not going to happen.

Over the past 30 years, I have learned that it is impossible to satisfy everybody. In fact, when you try to please everybody, it actually prevents you from truly pleasing anybody!

Let me change your life with this next thought: Somewhere out there lives your specific audience. These are the people you are assigned to reach. They are your audience.

My mentor, Michael Port, explained it to me this way: "There are some people you are meant to serve—and others, not so much." It is that simple.

Yes, we would all like to have a huge audience, but think of it this way: if you created the world's best-fried chicken recipe, you would not market it to folks who only ate baked turkey. If they do not care for what you are serving, it does not matter how delicious it is! Imagine what our lives could be if we spent less time worrying about the critics and focused our energy on the people we are truly called to serve!

The key to success in your career, your ministry, and your whole life is to find those people you were meant to serve. Then focus on them. Focus on those who value your gifts and your message.

Imagine waking up every day and sharing your ideas with people who are interested in them. And I am not talking only about your friends and family. I am talking about any people who share your passion in life—and believe that you have something that can add value to their lives!

I know; this vision of life sounds too good to be true. That is how it sounded to me only five years ago. I thought that the world was full of critics, just itching to tear down my dreams. Then something amazing happened for me.

I discovered my audience. You, because we are having a conversation right now via this book, are part of that audience. You are one of the individuals with whom I get to share my life and my dreams. You are important to me, and I value you. I value my audience!

Understanding Your Power

Every visionary needs to understand the power of conversation. A conversation can be more than a chat. A book is a conversation between an author and his or her readers. A sermon is a conversation between pastor and congregation.

A conversation, in all of its forms, has the power to make or break a life. Having the right conversations can set the tone for your future. That is because conversations shape our beliefs.

In **Romans 10:17,** the apostle Paul assures us that *"faith comes from what is heard."*

It is important to understand that "faith" means more than religious belief. The faith you need to accomplish anything in life comes from what you hear. This means that we must strive to hear the right things—to have the right conversations—to realize our dreams.

Do you know that your entire belief system has been formed by the conversations you have engaged in? Think about the talks you have had with people you trust. Think about the parents, grandparents, teachers, or other mentors who have worked together to shape your life by what they have taught you. Think about the conversations, the questions, answers, and the words of comfort and encouragement—especially at key moments in your life.

These conversations helped you discover who you are. They have established your vision for life.

The same can be said of the books you have read, the sermons you have heard, or the radio or TV ministries you have shared in. When I speak, I like to remind my audiences, "What you hear determines what you believe, and who you hear will determine what you will do."

Yes! The people who shape our belief systems are the people who shape our lives. They set our moral compass and form our outlook on life. Of course, this can be a good thing or a bad thing.

The people who influence our lives have the power to make or break our futures. They can encourage us on our journey of discovery or they can discourage us from chasing our vision. Just one conversation with someone you trust can alter the course of your life. Think deeply on this truth, and ask yourself, "In my life, am I having the right conversations with the right people?" Further, are the conversations I am having helping me to accomplish my life's goals?"

These questions are vital to realizing your dreams.

You can have the right conversation with the wrong person and lose your way on life's journey. This is why everyone must understand his or her audience. Do not take your right idea to the wrong audience. You could sink your own ship. You could lose faith in your vision.

The Bible puts it this way: *"Do not throw your pearls before hogs."* **(Matthew 7:6, AMP)**

In other words, do not give your goods to pigs. Some people will not want or understand your ideas. Do not let their negativity or lack of understanding undermine your faith in your message.

I often wonder what would have happened if Jesus had a conversation with the wrong people about His impending death on the cross. What if He talked with the disciples in the garden of Gethsemane? What if they tried to discourage Him? I can imagine Peter advising, "Master, are these fickle people really worth dying for? Most of them do not accept your message in the first place!"

There is a reason Jesus went off to pray alone. We can learn from His example. Let us never allow people to talk us out of making the right decision. Sometimes this means getting away from people and taking ourselves into the realm of private prayer.

Something powerful happened at Gethsemane. Like many visionary leaders on the brink of accomplishing a purpose, Jesus considered the task ahead of Him. He prayed to God, saying, "If it be thy will, let this cup pass from me." Consider those words. They are the words of someone who is exhausted, frightened, and tempted to give up.

I love Jesus's example here. He did not call a meeting with ministerial leaders or even His closest advisors. He took

Himself to a place of prayer. He had a personal but powerful conversation. He spoke intimately with His Heavenly Father. He took His "faith assignment" directly to the Source of that faith. He shared in the greatest conversation that any visionary can have. And He emerged from this conversation empowered, reassured, strengthened, and equipped to complete His mission.

Life's conversations will shape who you are. Be thoughtful about those who shape your message. And be thoughtful about the audience you will share that message with someday. Most of all, keep Jesus' example in mind. In life, the first and most important conversation to have is a conversation with God!

OUTRAGEOUS ACTIVITY:

1. *List the three people you talk to the most.*

    1. _______________________________

    2. _______________________________

    3. _______________________________

2. *Look back at the list. Are these people helping you or hurting you? If they are helping you, awesome. If not, it may be time to distance yourself from them.*

3. *Whom are you supposed to reach with your dream, gifts and purpose? Who is your audience?*

4. *List three strategies you will work on to reach the people who can benefit from your gifts and your dream:*

    1. _______________________________

    2. _______________________________

    3. _______________________________

5. **Now, go back and put timelines and dates beside those three items so you can be working your outrageous dream!**

CHAPTER 13

DEVOTIONS —5 FUNDAMENTAL TRUTHS FOR DREAMERS

DAY 1: Passion is the Fuel

Vision Verses

Romans 12:11 *Never be lacking in zeal, but keep your spiritual fervor, serving the Lord.*

Titus 2:14*...who gave himself for us to redeem us from all iniquity and to purify for himself a people of his own who are zealous for good deeds.*

1. Don't lose your passion (zeal) for striving toward excellence.

Manifesting a vision is extremely challenging. The walk of every visionary is filled with pitfalls and victories. It is truly a journey filled with ups and downs. When you are chasing any dream, it is imperative that you maintain high levels of passion.

Passion is a critical component of the success in the life of any organization. Why? The answer is that people don't follow or support you because of what you have to offer. They ultimately follow you because of "the why" which drives you to do what you do. A passion for excellence is directly connected to your why.

Have you ever been to a hotel that was supposed to be a 4- or 5-star hotel, one, moreover, that had bad customer service? If that has ever happened to you, do you remember how nice the room was? Do you remember how splendid the lobby was? Do you remember all the amenities in your bathroom or living space? Most people don't. I, on the other hand, never forget the experiences that I have in hotels. I would rather pay more to be comfortable than pay less and be absolutely miserable. Excellence is important, but it is often diluted because of the anemic passion of the person presenting it. You need people on your team who help you maintain your passion levels and possess a contagious zeal that ignites a fire in others to do the same.

As you push toward excellence in everything you do, remember that. The "What" is important, but the "why" is more important. No matter how tired you may be, there is no point in doing it if you are not going to do it well.

If you are going to make sure that you are always on your A-game, you need to keep your passion high. Passion is the fuel that keeps you going, even when your interest runs out. When your days are rough, your zeal should give you the push to keep going! Passion also keeps us focused in times of adversity. On days that you feel like giving up, passion will give you the push that helps you get through the day and lead you to victory. It is almost like a *Five-Hour Energy* drink. It gives you a boost to revive your energy when you become weak.

No matter what vision you have been given, there will be days when you just don't want to give your effort 100 percent. Those are the days that you have to dig deeply. On those days, you will have to draw on a power higher than yourself or your team. You should do all things as if you are doing them as a service to God because in the end, He will get the glory for the success of your business. You make our Father proud when you go the extra mile for clients who trust in your service.

We are made in His likeness, and nothing brings the Father glory like our exceeding in abundant excellence in every area we touch.

If you are feeling run down, or weary it is okay to rest. We have to remember that even God rested on the seventh day. If you are going to excel in the next dimension of your life, it is going to require that you do some things that you have never done to flow in an excellence you never have achieved. If the enemy can get you exhausted and cause you to run out of fuel, your light will get dim and eventually flicker out. That God rested on the seventh day proves that there is a time to work and a time to cease from working. If you are going to accomplish your purpose in the earth with a spirit of victory and excellence, you are going to have to make yourself relax, rest, shut down, and get the much needed sleep your body needs to rejuvenate itself for the tasks ahead.

The last thing that you may have to do is to make some adjustments in your personal and/or professional circle. When you are birthing a dream into fruition, there are only two types of people: people who help you push the dream out, Midwives so to speak, or people who cause you to miscarry. Get each face in your mind right now. You need to write down the names of those individuals one by one, place them in a category, and then decide how to reorganize the people in your life to help you fuel your passion chamber. You need every source of positive energy flowing into you as you prepare to go to this next level of greatness.

Vision Key Quote:

There are no neutral relationships. People are either armor bearers or pallbearers. They are either taking you to your destiny, or they are taking you to your grave.

–Pastor Van Moody

Vision Prayer:

Father God, I praise you and thank you for every time you have given me strength when I felt as if I could not make it. I truly have learned that when I am weak, you really are strong. I can run to you and find shelter; you protect from my enemies, and you hide me until I can recover and gain enough power to fight another day. As I take a time to reflect about the people around me, I ask that you give me the discernment and wisdom to recognize the people who are a life source to me and help refuel my passion and drive to succeed in abundant excellence. I also ask for the ability to see those who may need to be realigned in this season and be repositioned away from me. You are truly amazing; you never cease to astonish me with the knowledge you send my way at just the right time. I praise you for directing my paths as I continue to lean not to my own understanding and acknowledge you in all my ways. I thank you for this shift in my life. I thank you that as I get the rest I need and properly position my inner circle, you will strengthen me to pursue excellence and cause everything I touch to prosper exceedingly and abundantly beyond anything I could ask, dream, think, or imagine. I thank you in advance for doing it now, in Jesus' Name, Amen.

Vision Application

List Three Things That Drain Your Passion or Weaken Your Faith.

1. _______________________________________

2. _______________________________________

3. _______________________________________

List Three Things That Help Restore Your Passion/Faith (Or Have Restored it in the Past).

1. ______________________________

2. ______________________________

3. ______________________________

List three Adjustments That You Can Make To Your Routine to Get Better Rest.

1. ______________________________

2. ______________________________

3. ______________________________

DAY 2: Your Dream Lifeline is You

Vision Verses

Genesis 37:5 Joseph had a dream, and when he told it to his brothers, they hated him all the more.

James 2:26 As the body without the spirit is dead, so faith without deeds is dead.

2. You are the life of your dream; if you stop dreaming everything else stops.

Joseph is the model for every visionary. Despite all of the challenges that he had to endure, Joseph never stopped believing in his dream. You may ask, "How do we know that?" "How do we know that Joseph never stopped believing his dream?"

We know because no matter what happened to him, he always maintained his dignity and integrity. We know because every place that Joseph's foot trod was made better as a result of his being there. We know because no matter what his enemies did to him, nothing was able to prevent his dream from manifesting itself. We also know this because Joseph never stopped working. Faith without works is dead. In every chapter of Joseph's life, he was working. Your ability to keep believing and moving—in spite of what it looks like—determines the time of manifestation. Your dream will never manifest itself without faith in action.

We have to get to the place that we realize that the promises of God are "yes" and "amen." God has not changed His mind about what He promised us. The real question is, "Have I changed my mind about my dream?"

When God plants something within you, it may take a while to sprout. It may take a while for the roots to become established in the soul and the tree to break through the ground. But whether you can see it or not, it is happening. Every dream has a different recipe for it to bake properly and ultimately be what the master chef desires for it to become.

I am not sure if you have ever been to the home of someone who really cooks, not just any cook, but the type of cook who makes things from scratch. This is not a kitchen to enter into when you are hungry. Every inch of his or her meats is seasoned to perfection. Most of these people don't use measuring cups; they just follow their creative instincts. Or should I say that they use faith? They put extreme care into the meal that is being created, and when the dinner bell is rung, they believe that it is going to bless everyone who tastes it.

In the same way, when God gives you a dream, the amount of time that you spend nurturing and preparing for it will determine how that dream comes to fruition. But no matter how much you invest in it, the dream can't manifest itself if you stop believing!

Have you ever had a dream that you can barely remember? That happens when you passively dream it. It is the same action that happens when you watch a really funny movie, but later you can't remember any of the jokes. Or, it is like going to a church service and the pastor gives an awe-inspiring Word, but because you were only passively listening, you cannot recall much of it later.

Today, I want to encourage you to aggressively dream. When you are an aggressive dreamer, you work on your dream every day. Not one day passes that you aren't putting thought, activity, and energy toward your dream. You need all three if your dream is going to come alive. You need to think about it. "Every" action is the result of a thought that was first conceived in your mind. That is why the Word tells us to think of good things. Thinking good thoughts produces good actions. But thinking is not enough. That thinking has to turn into activity. No dream comes to pass without a flurry of activity. And it can't just be random actions! The activities that produce dreams are like the cook's meal that we were talking about before. The actions are deliberate, the actions are detail-oriented, and when the time comes to taste the results, the meal taste exactly the way the cook intends for it to taste. If you are cooking roast, you are not using the same seasonings that you use for jerk chicken. You have to use the right seasonings to get the right taste, and in the same way, you must use the right actions to get the right results. Last, you have or depressed. You have to get up everyday energized and ready to go. You must be determined to work your dream!

Vision Inspiration

"Hold fast to dreams,
For if dreams die
Life is a broken-winged bird,
That cannot fly."

-Langston Hughes

Vision Application

You must keep dreaming your dream until is comes to pass. Let's do the work to help it manifest.

Write down Two Thoughts that you need to Change.

1. ___________________________

2. ___________________________

Write down Two Thoughts that you need to Adopt.

1. ___________________________

2. ___________________________

Write down Three Activities that you need to do regularly to see your dream to manifest.

1. ____

2. ____

3. ____

Vision Vantage Point:

If you are going to have the energy you need to activate your dream, you need to make sure that you are getting the proper rest, nutrition, and exercise that you need. If you make these adjustments, you will find yourself soaring with an incredible amount of energy.

DAY 3: Don't Focus On The Small Things

Vision Verses

Galatians 6:9 Let us not become weary in doing good, for at the proper time we will reap a harvest if we do not give up. (NIV)

James 1:2 Consider it pure joy, my brothers and sisters, whenever you face trials of many kinds... (NIV)

3. Your Success is determined by what you are willing to ignore.

We are capable of allowing our dreams to drown out the distractions of life because we already practice this everyday. You don't turnaround and go back home because it starts raining. You turn on your windshield wipers, and you keep going.

When a driver darts out in front of you as if he or she is escaping from the police, only to get in front of you and drive at a snail's pace, you don't make a U-turn in the opposite direction and start going in the wrong direction just to get away from the slow driver.

In both of the instances, you handle the situation the way you have been taught. You put those windshield wipers on because in driver's education, someone taught you that. When you get behind a slow driver, you stay behind him or her until you get to a two-lane road where you can switch lanes or wait to get to a place in the road where the lines indicate that it is safe to pass, and then you pass the driver.

The same way you have to be flexible in everyday driving scenarios, you have to be able to replicate this same flexibility in your life. You cannot allow distractions to change your course of direction.

I once heard Bishop Jakes say, "You can wreck your car trying to swat a fly." Small things can take your focus off the main thing. Learning how to fix your eyes on the prize will help you to manifest your vision and avoid some of the frustration and negative pit stops.

Small situations/issues are sometimes the biggest hindrances of vision. These distractions consistently attempt to divert you from your plan. They seemingly can come out of nowhere, especially when you are vulnerable or not expecting them. They can be silent killers of your productivity, drive, hope, intentions, and plans. But you can't let them. Our vision verse reminds us that we should never become weary in our well doing for there is a reward ahead if we can only keep going.

Be determined to become a master of ignoring the insignificant happenings that can so easily throw you off your course.

Vision Application

What are the things that distract you most when you are attempting to accomplish your goals?

____

____

____

What are some things that you can do to protect yourself from becoming distracted by those things?

____

____

____

Are there some key people in your personal or professional circle who can assist you so that these issues are not as much of a challenge for you?

____

____

____

What are three goals that you are determined to make happen in the next thirty days?

1. ______________________________________

2. ______________________________________

3. ______________________________________

Vision Vantage Point:

If you allow yourself to become distracted by the small things, the big picture will become blurred.

DAY 4: Be True to the Authenticity of Your Own Dream

Vision Verses

John 8:32 And ye shall know the truth, and the truth shall make you free.

4. Don't allow people to label you or your dream.

One of the things fascinating about God is His intentionality in creating individuals. Even identical twins have different DNA, fingerprints, and voices. Even though God has the opportunity to create people who are almost alike in every way, there is still something about them that is unique to that individual.

If God was so intentional about making us originals, why do we work so hard to be copies or replicas of someone else?

Sometimes, this occurs because of a trauma or abuse that we have suffered. Sometimes, this happens as the result of abandonment or neglect. But often, it happens when we allow people to label us. Whether it is intentional or unintentional, another person's label can limit what you are able to accomplish.

When you accept the limit that was imposed upon you, it actually attaches itself to you and makes itself a part of your being. That label now has transformed you into someone other than whom your Creator designed and destined for you to be.

You may have been born on the other side of the tracks, but that geography doesn't have to define or limit you the rest of your life. You must be determined to shake off the labels and limits that have been imposed on you till this point of your life. One you are free from those chains, you can take the next big step in being true to authenticity of your own dream. You can stop compromising your own God-given vision for someone else's.

Today, I want you take the Authentic Dreamer's Affirmation:

Starting today, I will never let anyone else define my dream. After today, I will be everything that God said I can be. Right now, I shake off every chain that has shackled me through abuse, neglect, unforgiveness, name-calling, degrading remarks, abandonment, depression, and low self-esteem. From this day forward I promise God and myself that I will live authentically and be true to my dream.

I encourage you to say this every day until you mean it. Success follows only authentic dreamers. It is tempting to wish for the success of others and to, in a real way, imitate their efforts, both good and bad. You can become so infatuated with the lifestyle of people around you that you become obsessed with what, in fact, are their dreams. This can easily cause you to put your own dreams on hold; you might even dismiss your dream as inferior to theirs and begin to emulate the actions of people you really don't even know. If you can't be who you are, you most certainly cannot be who you aren't. You have been hiding in the shadows long enough; come and live your dream. It's time.

Vision Prayer:

Dear Heavenly Father: Before I request anything else from You, I ask for forgiveness. I repent for allowing myself to believe the enemy's lie that my best was not enough. I am sorry for every dream that I put in the trashcan to cultivate the field of dreams of someone else because I didn't believe in my own dream enough. I thank you for every field in which I have toiled and helped harvest the dreams of others. I pray that you bless me with the same success that I have helped provide for others. As I have been a loyal servant over others' companies and individual visions, I ask that you would now send loyal men and women to help me bring my vision to pass. I am grateful for this new revelation. I am grateful that I can start today by dreaming again. I praise you for my authentic dream and my authentic life that is only made possible by the shedding of blood of your only begotten Son, whom You sought fit to come and face death in my place, so that I may have the right to the tree of life. I will not shame you in the affairs of this life. I will run my race on this side of glory, while earning my crown on the other side. I am forever grateful that you loved me enough to give me wisdom, knowledge and the revelation of who I am in You. I will never be put to shame because I call on your Name. You are my Rock, My Shield, and because of you, I can do all things through You Who gives me the strength to do this. When you make my name great and allow me to be generous on every occasion, I will never forget that it is You and only You who have given me the ability to obtain wealth through pursuing my dreams and visions. I will be so careful to give all glory and praise to You. In Jesus' Mighty and Precious Name I Pray. Amen.

____

____

____

Vision Vantage Point:

Never forget, even though we were created by an all-powerful God; He saw fit to make every single one of us an original—to forsake your originality is an insult to your Creator. You owe it to Him to live authentically!

DAY 5: Your Dream Will Work—If You Work It

Vision Verses

James 2:17-18 In the same way, faith by itself, if it is not accompanied by action, is dead.

But someone will say, "You have faith; I have deeds. Show me your faith without deeds, and I will show you my faith by my deeds. (NIV)

5. "All our dreams can come true, if we have the courage to pursue them." –Walt Disney

Have you ever been in the store and watched parents with their children or this may have happened to you if you have children yourself...the parent is putting items on the register, and is counting the costs of every item going across the scanner? It seems that the parent has a set budget for the amount of items that he or she has placed in his or her cart. Yet there is a child standing nearby trying to get the parent to buy something that is completely not on his or her list. It may be a ring pop, it may be a magazine, it may be a candy bar, but that item is not on the parent's radar at all because it is not on the list.

Often, we adult believers associate with lack so much that we treat God as though He is the parent at the register, but we don't respond with the faith of the child. We treat God as if He has only a set amount of blessings that He can give us. We treat Him as if He is standing there counting how many miracles He has given out today, and He can't give out anymore. God wants us to treat Him the same way the child treats the parent. The child has no idea that there is a limit; the child just believes that the parent can get him or her whatever he or she wants. Well, in our case, our Father can! He just wants us to believe and back up our belief with our positive actions.

If you never pursue your dream, there is a guarantee that you will never see it. Back to our original example: some parents deny the request of the child because the child's desire isn't in their budget or on their list, but often, a parent will sacrifice one of the items in the cart or dig up some extra change for the additional purchase that the child has requested. The first rule of dreaming is doing. You have not because you ask not. You have to get out there and start moving. There is no time to waste. You can't sit around and idly wait for it. You wait for the bus, you wait for your car's oil to get changed at the dealership, you wait your turn at the doctor's office, but you don't wait for your dream. Your life can't be an incidental endeavor. People kill their dreams because they don't have the courage to step out in the effort to actualize them or bring them to any kind of semblance of reality. You have to be deliberate about your dream. One way to jumpstart your dream is to stop doing what you hate. People go through life trying to pursue things that they were never designed to pursue, because they have concluded that this is the "Plan of God" for their life, but that thing brings them no fulfillment and no joy. If you have been living this way, I am coming with good news. You don't have to live a life and pursue a career that you don't enjoy. God wired us to be connected to our purpose. It should actually be something that you enjoy doing. When you love what you do, it almost doesn't feel like work. I encourage you today to pursue your dream with everything within you. Your Father is not limited like the parent in the beginning of the story. Your Father owns the cattle on a thousand hills. Now, it is your job to trust like the child: ask your Father for what you need, and then be bold enough to pursue your dream today.

Vision Application

What are you passionate about? What gets you excited? What drives you?

What do you enjoy doing so much that if you could afford to, you would do it for free?

What is hindering you from pursuing your passion?

____

____

____

After reading this devotion and answering these questions, what are your next steps to bring about the necessary changes in your life? If you are actively pursuing your vision, who in your life does this chapter apply to? How are you going to try and help them?

____

____

____

____

____

Vision Vantage Point:

One of the greatest misconceptions about purpose is that God creates us to do things we **don't** enjoy doing. A good way to disprove this notion is to stand out as a shining example of one who is fulfilling your purpose!

Final Note:

Do not let your dream die. There is someone in the Earth waiting on you to fulfill your dream, use your gifts, and empower the world around you! There is greatness in you and this is the season, time, and purpose to walk it out.

I can't wait to hear your stories and see the amazing things you will do!

Let's stay connected.—JM Foster